❋Ephesians

DISCOVER TOGETHER BIBLE STUDY SERIES

Leader's guides are available at www.discovertogetherseries.com

A *Discover Together* BIBLE STUDY

Ephesians

Discovering Your Identity and Purpose in Christ

Sue Edwards

Kregel
Publications

Ephesians: Discovering Your Identity and Purpose in Christ
© 2012 by Sue Edwards

Published by Kregel Publications, a division of Kregel, Inc., P.O. Box 2607, Grand Rapids, MI 49501.

Previously published by Kregel Publications as *Ephesians: Finding Your Identity and Purpose in Christ*, © 2007 by Sue Edwards.

ISBN 978-0-8254-4309-1

Printed in the United States of America

12 13 14 15 16 / 5 4 3 2 1

Contents

How to Get the Most Out of a Discover Together Bible Study

W omen today need Bible study to keep balanced, focused, and Christ-centered in their busy worlds. The tiered questions in *Ephesians: Discovering Your Identity and Purpose in Christ* allow you to choose a depth of study that fits your lifestyle, which may even vary from week to week, depending on your schedule.

Just completing the basic questions will require about one and a half hours per lesson, and will provide a basic overview of the text. For busy women, this level offers in-depth Bible study with a minimum time commitment.

"Digging Deeper" questions are for those who want to, and make time to, probe the text even more deeply. Answering these questions may require outside resources such as an atlas, Bible dictionary, or concordance; you may be asked to look up parallel passages for additional insight; or you may be encouraged to investigate the passage using an interlinear Greek-English text or *Vine's Expository Dictionary*. This deeper study will challenge you to learn more about the history, culture, and geography related to the Bible, and to grapple with complex theological issues and differing views. Some with teaching gifts and an interest in advanced academics will enjoy exploring the depths of a passage, and might even find themselves creating outlines and charts and writing essays worthy of seminarians!

This inductive Bible study is designed for both individual and group discovery. You will benefit most if you tackle each week's lesson on your own, and then meet with other women to share insights, struggles, and aha moments. Bible study leaders will find free, downloadable leader's guides for each study, along with general tips for leading small groups, at www.discovertogetherseries.com.

Through short video clips, Sue Edwards shares personal insights to enrich your Bible study experience. You can watch these as you work through each lesson on your own, or your Bible study leader may want your whole

study group to view them when you meet together. For ease of individual viewing, a QR code, which you can simply scan with your smartphone, is provided in each lesson. Or you can go to www.discovertogetherseries.com and easily navigate until you find the corresponding video title. Woman-to-woman, these clips are meant to bless, encourage, and challenge you in your daily walk.

Each lesson also includes short teaching clips that are available to view at www.discoveryseries.net. You can view these as you work through each lesson on your own, or your Bible study leader may want your whole study group to view them when you meet together. For ease of individual viewing, a QR code is provided for each clip, which you can simply scan with your smartphone. Or you can go to the and easily navigate until you find the corresponding video title. Woman-to-woman, these clips are meant to bless, encourage, and challenge you in your daily walk.

Choose a realistic level of Bible study that fits your schedule. You may want to finish the basic questions first, and then "dig deeper" as time permits. Take time to savor the questions, and don't rush through the application. Watch the videos. Read the sidebars for additional insight to enrich the experience. Note the optional passage to memorize and determine if this discipline would be helpful for you. Do not allow yourself to be intimidated by women who have more time or who are gifted differently.

Make your Bible study—whatever level you choose—top priority. Consider spacing your study throughout the week so that you can take time to ponder and meditate on what the Holy Spirit is teaching you. Do not make other appointments during the group Bible study. Ask God to enable you to attend faithfully. Come with an excitement to learn from others and a desire to share yourself and your journey. Give it your best, and God promises to join you on this adventure that can change your life.

Why Study Ephesians?

Who are you? If someone asked you that, what would you say? Would you list your relationships or your abilities? Those are important components of your life, but they don't fully answer the question. What if those relationships ended? What if you lost that ability? Would you still be *you*? Paul wrote Ephesians to help us discover who we are in Jesus Christ and what God created each of us to do on this earth, an identity and purpose we can never lose. When you unearth those personal treasures, hold on! Your life will never be the same.

 Introduction to Studying Ephesians *(8:36 minutes)*

HISTORICAL BACKGROUND

Paul planted a church in Ephesus on his third missionary journey. After three years in Ephesus, he returned to Jerusalem, where he was taken prisoner and later transported to Rome to stand trial. In A.D. 61, while under house arrest in Rome, Paul wrote a letter to his beloved Ephesians.

Ephesus was the grandest city in Asia, and God chose to plant a church there because of its strategic location. The economy was booming, making Ephesus an international trade center. Tourists flocked from all over the Roman Empire. They came to see the outdoor theater, which seated 25,000 people, and the Temple of Artemis, which housed the thirty-seven-breasted fertility goddess. Under Artemis's perverse influence, sex was big business in this red-light city of public baths, cult prostitution, homosexuality, and bestiality.

Like many American cities today, people of all cultures and ethnic backgrounds called this metropolis home. Large Greek, Roman, and Jewish settlements had taken root, and each worshipped differently. Converts to the church came from diverse ethnic groups, making harmony a challenge.

Under Artemis's influence, the Ephesians incorporated black magic into their religion. As a result, Ephesus was known as the Roman Empire's stronghold for the occult and magical arts. When Paul planted a church in Ephesus, he knew he was invading Satan's den. This letter contains numerous references to spiritual warfare. Remember that when Paul wrote this letter, the Ephesians were only six years old in the Lord, and many were saved out of the occult. If the Ephesians learned to live victoriously, so can we!

Learn to Sit

A t the instant you ask Jesus to redeem you, you have everything you need to live a victorious Christian life! Paul says so in the first fourteen verses of this letter. Then why do so many of us struggle with the same sins over and over? Why do we seem impotent? Because we don't know who we are! Let's find out!

Pray before you begin the lesson. Ask the Holy Spirit to reveal your true identity in Christ, enabling you to be an overcomer.

 Read Ephesians 1:1–14.

 Spiritual Blessings (*3:47 minutes*). What does it mean to be blessed in the heavenly realms? Have a seat and bask in this life-changing truth.

THE GREETING

1. How does Paul describe himself in the opening phrase of the letter? Why is he the bearer of this title? (1:1)

OPTIONAL

Memorize Ephesians 1:3

Praise be to the God and Father of our Lord Jesus Christ, who has blessed us in the heavenly realms with every spiritual blessing in Christ.

The individual Christian life begins with a man "in Christ"—that is to say, when by faith we see ourselves seated together with him in the heavens. Most Christians make the mistake of trying to walk in order to be able to sit, but that is a reversal of the true order. . . . If at the outset we try to do anything, we get nothing; if we seek to attain something, we miss everything. For Christianity begins not with a big DO, but with a big DONE.
—Watchman Nee
(*Sit, Walk, Stand*, 14)

2. How does he describe the Ephesians (1:l)? Why might it be difficult to live this way in a city like Ephesus? (See the historical background information in "Why Study Ephesians?")

3. Verse 2 is a combination of two familiar Ephesian greetings: "grace" by the Greeks and "peace" by the Jews. How would you define *grace* and *peace*? Have you experienced one or both? If so, what difference do grace and peace make in your life?

4. Why is Paul praising God in verse 3?

In the original Greek, verses three through fourteen constitute one single complex sentence.

When I read verses three through fourteen, I hear a symphony of blessings serenading God's beloved. If you have never been serenaded, sit back and rest in this beautiful sonata that sings truth about you if you are *in Christ*. —Sue

5. What do you think it means to be "blessed . . . in the heavenly realms"? See Ephesians 1:20–21 and 2:6–7 for additional insight.

The bird is in the air; the
  air is in the bird.
The fish is in the water; the
  water is in the fish.
The iron is in the fire; the
  fire is in the iron.
The believer is in Christ and
  Christ is in the believer.
      —J. Vernon McGee
        (*Ephesians*, 20)

You are in the heavenlies in Christ even when you are down in the dumps. Everyone who is in Christ is seated in the heavenlies in Him. That is the position which He has given us.
      —J. Vernon McGee
        (*Ephesians*, 23)

Paul now lists our spiritual blessings. If you belong to Christ, these verses are true about you!

6. When were the Ephesians chosen to belong to God, and when were you chosen (1:4a)?

7. What were you chosen to be, and how does God view you now (1:4b)? Do you *really* believe this is your position in Christ? If not, why not? If so, what difference does this understanding make in the way you live?

8. Verse 5 reveals that you have been adopted by God. According to the verse, why did God do this?

9. What does it mean to be adopted? What does Galatians 3:26–29 explain about our spiritual adoption? If you have personal experience with adoption, please share your insight with the group.

10. What happened to make your blessing and position possible and secure (Ephesians 1:6–8)?

11. What words or phrases in Ephesians 1:6–8 reveal Paul's emotions as he is writing? How do you think he is feeling?

A GREAT MYSTERY

A *mystery* in the New Testament is a truth that was not previously understood but is now being revealed. Paul now writes concerning the end of history and our destiny.

12. What mystery is revealed (1:9–10)? When do you think this will happen?

13. In verse 11, Paul reiterates that believers were chosen according to God's preordained plan. As a result of being chosen, what does God say is the Christian's purpose in life (1:12)?

14. What is your specific purpose in life? Is it in accordance with God's general will for you as stated in verse 12?

How we need to lay hold of Him today and to start living as a child of God should live!
—J. Vernon McGee
(*Ephesians*, 25)

DIGGING DEEPER

Several times in 1:3–14, Paul says believers were "chosen" and "predestined" to become God's children. Then in verse 13, he says the Ephesians became Christians when they heard and believed the gospel. Belief implies a decision freely made. How can both statements be true? Do an in-depth study on predestination and free will. See Romans chapters 9–11. For insight, read *Evangelism and the Sovereignty of God* by J. I. Packer.

15. How have you been marked by God and sealed eternally (1:13)? How does this gift manifest himself in your life?

If I say, "I will not mention him, or speak any more in his name," then within me there is something like a burning fire shut up in my bones; I am weary with holding it in, and I cannot. (Jeremiah 20:9)

There is something like that in all of us—something so essential to who we are and who God made us to be that we cannot set it aside without imploding.
—Ruth Haley Barton
(*Sacred Rhythms*, 123)

16. When you make a business transaction such as purchasing a home, you put down nonrefundable earnest money to assure the seller that you will go through with the transaction. How does verse 14 picture this transaction in spiritual terms? Who has purchased you and owns you now?

We need nothing less than a new reformation and Ephesians is the document to bring it about. This short little letter is a surprisingly comprehensive statement about God and his work, about Christ and the gospel, about life with God's Spirit, and about the right way to live.
—Klyne Snodgrass
(*Ephesians*, 18)

DIGGING DEEPER

List evidences you find for the doctrine of the Trinity in Ephesians 1:1–14.

17. From 1:3–14, what blessings and benefits do you enjoy as a Christian? How do you feel as you contemplate what God has done and will do for you?

18. What are some ways to thank God now?

[Ephesians] certainly is the most spiritual and devout, composed in an exalted and transcendent state of mind, where theology rises into worship and meditation into oration. It is the Epistle of the Heavenlies. . . . The aged apostle soared high above all earthly things to the invisible and eternal realities in heaven. From his gloomy confinement he ascended for a season to the mount of transfiguration. The prisoner of Christ, chained to a pagan soldier, was transformed into a conqueror, clad in the panoply of God, and singing a paean of victory.
—Philip Schaff (*History*, 780)

19. Paul writes that these blessings mark and identify us as God's children. How do you see yourself? What factors have you allowed to shape your identity? Are these factors from the world or from God's Word?

20. In light of Ephesians 1:3–14, who are you? Are you living up to who you are? Why or why not? What can you do to live up to your identity?

21. Are there any comments or questions you would like to add to the discussion?

DIGGING DEEPER

Read through Ephesians in one sitting. Label the sections. What general themes can you identify? What do you think is the main theme of the book? For historical background on the city of Ephesus, read *Power and Magic: The Concept of Power in Ephesians* by Clinton Arnold.

Sit and Pray

LESSON 2

This lesson is not about praying for a specified time each day. Daily devotions are admirable but they do not guarantee victory in our trials. It is possible to pray several hours each morning and forget God the rest of the day. God asks us to live in a constant attitude of prayer. What does that mean? When we live in an attitude of prayer, we include God in the inner conversations of our hearts and minds all day long. We include God as we carry out our daily routines, and we bring God into all our relationships. We live seated in him, resting in his enablement, every minute.

Paul was a man of prayer. He spent blocks of time in prayer and he lived the remaining hours resting in Christ—even when he was busy for the Lord. Pray for insight into Paul's two prayers, one in Ephesians 1:15–23 and the other in 3:14–21. Ask, as the disciples asked, "Lord, teach us to pray" (Luke 11:1).

TAKING STOCK

1. We talk about prayer, but do we really pray? Analyze your prayer life. Remember we are not just concerned with blocks of time set aside to pray, but also a prayer attitude we take with us through our day.

OPTIONAL

Memorize Ephesians
3:17b–19

I pray that you, being rooted and established in love, may have power, together with all the Lord's holy people, to grasp how wide and long and high and deep is the love of Christ, and to know this love that surpasses knowledge— that you may be filled to the measure of all the fullness of God.

Paul has praised God for his magnificent blessings available to every Christian. Now he prays that we will open our eyes to grasp and appreciate the fullness of these blessings, and then live in that reality.   —Sue

2. What hinders you from living a life of prayer? Be honest, and refuse to take a guilt trip. Many Christians struggle with prayer. When do you tend to forget God and rely on yourself?

3. (*Optional*) On the last pages of this lesson (pages 36–37) is a prayer log to help you gain insight into your prayer life. Record times you pray and your heart attitude the rest of the day. Do not compare yourself with others. Seek progress in your own life.

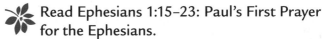 **Read Ephesians 1:15–23: Paul's First Prayer for the Ephesians.**

KNOWING GOD

4. What were the Ephesians known for (1:15)? How did Paul express his love for them (1:16)?

5. In our small groups, we often want to solve one another's problems by giving advice or explaining what worked for us. Although this may be helpful, what is the best thing we can do for a struggling sister? Why?

6. According to Ephesians 1:17, what is Paul's ongoing, number one prayer for the Ephesians, and what will result? Why is this top priority?

The apostle prays the lights will go on inside people so that they know God and understand the benefits of the gospel.
—Klyne Snodgrass
(*Ephesians*, 73)

Define *wisdom* and *revelation* as these terms are used in the context of verse 17. How might wisdom and revelation help you know God more intimately?

7. How well do you *really* know God? What has helped you know him better? What part does prayer play?

THE EYES OF YOUR HEART

God measures everything, from start to finish, by the perfections of his Son. Scripture clearly affirms that it is God's good pleasure "to sum up all things in Christ . . . in whom also we were made a heritage" (Eph. 1:9–11). It is my earnest prayer that . . . our eyes may be opened afresh to see that it is only by placing our entire emphasis *there* that we can hope to realize the divine purpose for us, which is that "we should be unto the praise of his glory" (1:12).
　　　　—Watchman Nee
　　(*Sit, Walk, Stand*, 9–10)

8. What else does Paul pray for the Ephesians in 1:18a? What do you think this means? Have you experienced this? Can you give an example? If so, please share.

9. When the "eyes of your heart are enlightened," Paul says you will understand several significant truths about your life and future. List them.

Ephesians 1:18

Ephesians 1:19

The mind alone cannot grasp the truth of God; the heart of man, his affections and especially his will, must all be bent to the task. Otherwise the essential part of divine revelation will escape the student, leaving only an unsatisfying and incomprehensible framework within his grasp. In this lies the explanation of much barren intellectual study of Scripture.
—Alexander Ross ("Pauline Epistles," 1019)

10. What do the following verses tell us about "the hope to which God has called you" (1:18)? Do you *really* believe that what is revealed in these passages will happen to you?

Romans 8:18–19, 23–25

1 Corinthians 15:19–23

1 John 3:1–3

11. Do you pray with hope and expectation? How might an understanding of your future hope affect the way you pray?

12. *Review.* When the eyes of your heart are opened, Paul says you will understand your inheritance (1:18). Name the riches already revealed in 1:3–14. Are you living like an heir or like a pauper?

13. Paul also says when your spiritual eyes are opened, you will understand "his incomparably great power." What kind of "incomparably great power" is Paul talking about in verse 19? (Meditate on 1:19b–20.)

 Resurrection Power (*4:18 minutes*). One of our incomparable blessings in Christ is resurrection power. Imagine what this power can do in our lives!

14. How could this vast resource make a significant difference in the way you handle trials and struggles? Can you recall an experience when you tapped into this power source and were amazed at the results? If so, please share.

> The very same resurrection power which God exhibited in Christ is now available for us.
> —John Stott (*Message*, 67)

15. How could this vast resource make a difference in the way you pray?

16. What is Christ's position and authority (1:20–23)?

17. In what sense is his reign yet to be realized? Is the honor and homage due him a reality today? What part can you play to make it a reality?

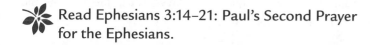 Read Ephesians 3:14–21: Paul's Second Prayer for the Ephesians.

HIS GLORIOUS RICHES

18. What physical position does Paul take as he prays (3:14)? What does this reveal about his heart attitude? Have you ever prayed kneeling or lying on the floor? If so, how did you feel?

> This is the second great prayer of Paul in this epistle. As he viewed the church as the poem of God, the temple of the Holy Spirit, the mystery of the ages, he went to God in prayer that these great truths might become realities in the lives of believers.
> —J. Vernon McGee
> (*Ephesians*, 100)

19. Paul repeats many of the same concepts in both prayers. What elements in 3:16–17 are a repetition of 1:17–19? Why do you think Paul repeats himself?

> God's power does not remove us from persecution, danger, difficulty, and death, but makes us more than conquerors in all such things. This is not a power to work magic and escape difficulty, but a power to live in an evil world. This power is for godly living.
> —Klyne Snodgrass
> (*Ephesians*, 92)

20. Now Paul makes a new request as he prays. What does he want the Ephesians to grasp? Why (3:17–19)?

21. What do you think it means to be filled with God's fullness? How might a dynamic and consistent prayer life help you be filled with God's fullness?

22. Is God's love real to you? Why or why not? Do you understand its vastness? Why is it critical that you grasp his vast love as you pray and deal with life?

23. Verses 20–21 are called a doxology or a benediction, often recited to conclude a church service. What is God able to do in you?

24. What do you need him to do right now that is "immeasurably more than all we ask or imagine"? Where do these miracles take place (3:20)? Are you asking, or trying to make things happen yourself?

25. As God works out his plan in history, what will result (3:21)?

26. What have you learned about prayer from the lesson or from someone in your group that will help you live a life of prayer?

Prayer is not *you* trying to move *God*. Prayer is among other things *being caught up* into God's directions and activity. He orders the affairs of the universe, and he invites you to participate by prayer. Intercession is God and you in partnership, bringing his perfect plans into being.
—John White (*The Fight*, 27)

DIGGING DEEPER

Study the great prayers of Scripture listed below. Compare and contrast these prayers. What do you learn?

· Hannah's prayer in 1 Samuel 2
· David's prayer in 2 Samuel 7:18–29
· Solomon's prayer in 1 Kings 8:23–53
· Nehemiah's prayer in Nehemiah 1
· Isaiah's prayer in Isaiah 6
· Daniel's prayer in Daniel 9
· Jesus' prayers in Luke 11 and John 17
· Paul's prayer in Philippians 1:3–11

MY PRAYER LOG

Sunday   Time spent talking to God: _____

Today my heart and mind were close to God. Yes _____ No _____

I lost touch with God today when _____

The lesson God taught me today was _____

_____

Monday   Time spent talking to God: _____

Today my heart and mind were close to God. Yes _____ No _____

I lost touch with God today when _____

The lesson God taught me today was _____

_____

Tuesday   Time spent talking to God: _____

Today my heart and mind were close to God. Yes _____ No _____

I lost touch with God today when _____

The lesson God taught me today was _____

_____

Wednesday Time spent talking to God: _____

Today my heart and mind were close to God. Yes _____ No _____

I lost touch with God today when _____

The lesson God taught me today was _____

_____

Thursday   Time spent talking to God: _____

Today my heart and mind were close to God. Yes _____ No _____

I lost touch with God today when _____

The lesson God taught me today was _____

_____

Friday   Time spent talking to God: _____

Today my heart and mind were close to God. Yes _____ No _____

I lost touch with God today when _____

The lesson God taught me today was _____

_____

Saturday   Time spent talking to God: _____

Today my heart and mind were close to God. Yes _____ No _____

I lost touch with God today when _____

The lesson God taught me today was _____

_____

Sit Down to Work

The instant you become a Christian, you are transformed into a new person. God does it all! And he enables you to live in a completely new way. But you must learn to live resting in him, even when you are working. Even your good works are his because you are his handiwork (2:10).

This week, ask God to point out times when you try to live in your own strength—and ask him to show you how to rest in him. When you learn to sit down in Christ, you will find energy and strength "to do immeasurably more than all you could ask or imagine."

 Read Ephesians 2:1–10.

YOUR FORMER LIFE

1. How does Paul characterize you before you knew Christ (2:1)? Note the verb tense.

In order to experience true transformation, I need to decide what I believe and why I believe it. Then I need to figure out a way to live according to those beliefs.
—Nancy Ortberg
(*Looking for God*, 177)

The Greek word "disobedient" in verse 2 is *apeitheia*, where we get our word *apathetic*. A better translation is "unbelieving" or "unpersuadable."

DIGGING DEEPER

What do you think Paul means by the term *world* (2:2)? What do the following verses tell you about the world?

· 1 Corinthians 1:18–31

· Galatians 6:14

· 1 John 2:15–16

· 1 John 5:5, 10–12

DIGGING DEEPER

Who is "the ruler of the kingdom of the air"? What do the following verses tell you about him?

· Isaiah 14:12–15

· 1 Peter 5:8–10

· 1 John 4:4

2. What two forces dominated your life before you came to faith (2:2)?

3. How does Paul say he and the Ephesians acted before they came to faith (2:3)?

4. What was your life like during those unregenerate years?

THE WAR WITHIN

5. If God transformed us when we came to faith in Christ, why do we sometimes still act the way we did before we came to faith? What is going on within us? (See Romans 7:21–25; James 4:1; and 1 Peter 2:11.)

DIGGING DEEPER

Study Galatians 5:13–26 for more insight into the spiritual battle within. What is the only way to conquer our sinful nature?

Religion can tempt us to do a little behavioral modification on ourselves. Internal transformation can be so much work and so difficult to measure that it is easier to just clean up and conform on the outside. But all that work on the outside can fool us into thinking that the inside is being taken care of as well.
—Nancy Ortberg
(*Looking for God*, 174–75)

6. Who is winning the spiritual battle within you right now? Why? What can you do to help God win this internal struggle? Be specific.

Spiritual Warfare (*5:14 minutes*). What is our vantage point as spiritual warfare is waged? Sue explains.

LIFE IN CHRIST

7. According to the first part of Ephesians 2:5, what did God do for you the moment you came to faith? Why (2:4)?

8. According to Ephesians 2:6, what else did God do for you? What does this mean?

9. Why did God make us alive, raise us up, and seat us with Christ? Why is it wrong to try to earn salvation by good works? What are we attempting to take away from God that is due him and him alone (2:7)?

God sovereignly bestows the gift of eternal life on the sinner at the moment he believes and thereby declares him righteous while the sinner still lives a life marked by periodic sinfulness. He hasn't joined a church. He hasn't started paying tithes. He hasn't given up all to follow Christ. He hasn't been baptized. He hasn't promised to live a sacrificial, spotlessly pure life. He has simply taken the gift of eternal life. He has changed his mind toward Christ (repentance) and accepted the free gift of God apart from works. Period. Transaction completed. By grace, through faith alone, God declares the sinner righteous (justification) and from that moment on the justified sinner begins a process of growth toward maturity (sanctification).
—Charles Swindoll
(*Grace Awakening*, 42)

10. Paul writes, "It is by grace you have been saved, . . . it is the gift of God—not by works, so that no one can boast" (2:8–9). Define *grace*.

GOD'S MASTERPIECE

What are we now? We are God's *workmanship* (*poiema*, his work of art, his masterpiece) *created* (*ktisthentes*) *in Christ Jesus*. Both Greek words speak of creation . . . and each declares that the work is God's, for dead people cannot bring themselves to life again, nor can captive and condemned people free themselves. . . . Salvation is creation, re-creation, new creation.
    —John Stott (*Message*, 84)

11. From Ephesians 2:10, what does Paul call us and what is one of the reasons God saved us?

12. What do you think it means that God prepared your good works in advance for you to do?

> But by the grace of God I am what I am, and his grace to me was not without effect. No, I worked harder than all of them—yet not I, but the grace of God that was with me.
> —The apostle Paul, 1 Corinthians 15:10

13. If your good works will never earn you God's salvation or love, what is their purpose? (See Matthew 5:16; John 9:1–3; Ephesians 1:12; 2:10; and Titus 3:8.)

Ephesians 2:10 shows salvation is not from works, but it is *for* good works. God saves people so that they might live productive lives in keeping with what God intended for humanity. With "good works" Paul was not thinking about "do-goodism," but about a life reflective of God's love.
—Klyne Snodgrass
(*Ephesians*, 121)

14. How will good works benefit you in the future? (See 1 Corinthians 3:10–15; Ephesians 6:8; Colossians 3:24; and Revelation 22:12.)

15. What good works has God prepared for you to do? Are you doing them? If not, why not? If serving God has brought you joy, please share this experience with the group.

16. Have you tried to do good works in your own strength? If so, what happened? If you have learned to work while "seated with Christ in the heavenlies," share the benefits with the group.

Sit Down Together

The church in Ephesus was composed of different ethnic groups. Some were former Jews who tended to be critical, stodgy, and legalistic. Others left pagan Artemis worship to join the church. Their former lives smacked of occult worship, sexual promiscuity, and superstition. These two groups looked at life from totally different perspectives. But if they could not find a way to love one another and work together, the church at Ephesus could not stand. Paul writes encouraging words to help them, knowing that unity only comes through God's enabling power.

Has God brought you together with people who are different from you? They may be in your family, workplace, or church. Are you able to appreciate their differences, love them unconditionally, and work in harmony? God desired unity for the Ephesians and for us as well. Pray and ask him to show you how to enjoy the diverse people he has placed in your life.

 Read Ephesians 2:11–22.

THE PEACEMAKER

1. Both Ephesian Jews and Gentiles left their former religions to follow Christ. Now they were brothers and sisters. The former Jews, however, were probably excluding the Gentiles on the basis of their race and their past. What did Paul say to comfort the Gentiles (2:11–13)?

OPTIONAL

Memorize Ephesians 2:22

In him you too are being built together to become a dwelling in which God lives by his Spirit.

About three years before Paul wrote this letter, he was arrested in Jerusalem on the charge that he had taken an Ephesian Gentile named Trophimus into the restricted temple area (Acts 21:27–31).

Notice how frequently the text keeps alternating between the pronouns you and we. In this passage, when Paul writes you, he usually refers to Gentile Christians. When he writes we, he generally means Jewish believers. —Sue

A literal stone wall divided the temple in Jerusalem. It marked where Gentiles could not go, under penalty of death. The Jewish converts in the Ephesian church had continued to exclude Gentile converts out of habit, but God would not stand for it.

2. Who alone could enable these two groups to overcome their dislike for one another? What has he done? (2:14)

There is neither Jew nor Greek, neither slave nor free, nor is there male and female, for you are all one in Christ Jesus.
—Galatians 3:28

3. What kinds of "barriers" divide people in families, communities, nations, and the church today?

4. What barriers have you erected in your own life? Do you tend to assume that because someone is different, he or she is wrong? What differences in people irritate you the most (driving habits, decision making, spending habits, dress preferences, the direction of the toilet paper roll, etc.)?

 Called to Unity (*4:53 minutes*). God calls us to sit down together with people unlike us and link arms for the cause of Christ. How are we doing?

If the plight was estrangement and distance, the solution is nearness and belonging.
—Klyne Snodgrass
(*Ephesians*, 128)

5. These Ephesian believers were also separated on the basis of race and tradition. Name as many groups as you can that are divided for similar reasons. (Please do not mention specific denominations.)

The Jew had an immense contempt for the Gentile. . . . The barrier between them was absolute. If a Jewish boy married a Gentile girl, or if a Jewish girl married a Gentile boy, the funeral of that Jewish boy or girl was carried out. Such contact with a Gentile was the equivalent of death.
—William Barclay
(*Letters*, 125)

6. Do you dislike anyone on the basis of race, culture, or tradition? If so, why do you react this way? Discuss honestly and graciously. (Remember, no names please.)

7. Specifically, what did Christ do to make reconciliation and harmony possible for his people (2:15–16)?

When Paul says Christ "set aside" or "abolished" the law, he doesn't mean that the Old Testament is no longer the Word of God or a moral guide. What is abolished is the law as a set of regulations that exclude Gentiles. Other parts of the Old Testament law have been fulfilled by Christ, including the sacrificial system, which is no longer needed since Christ is the sacrifice for sins, once and for all (Hebrews 10:11–14). —Sue

8. How did his "setting aside" the law help us love one another and work together?

9. Why do you think Paul says that it is through the cross we are able to unite (2:16)?

10. What benefits do we enjoy together that help us overcome our differences (2:18)?

THE NEW FAMILY

Here there is no Gentile
or Jew, circumcised or
uncircumcised, barbarian,
Scythian, slave or free, but
Christ is all, and is in all.
—Colossians 3:11

11. What encouraging words did Paul write to the Gentiles in 2:19? If you are feeling excluded, how might these words comfort you?

12. If you tend to exclude others, what is the lesson for you in verse 19?

13. In 2:20–22, Paul paints a picture of what God wants the church to become. Who is the foundation of the church? What did they do and what did they leave us that make this statement true?

14. Who is the chief cornerstone of the church?

People are incorporated into [Jesus Christ], and when he is raised to new life, a new being comes into existence, one in which people are one with Christ and one with each other in him. Grace not only connects us to God and Christ, it connects us to each other.
—Klyne Snodgrass
(*Ephesians*, 134)

DIGGING DEEPER

Peter uses similar language to describe the united church. Study 1 Peter 2:4–10. Compare this section with Ephesians 2:20–22.

15. What happens when the whole building joins together (2:21–22)? Who are the bricks of the building? Who enables us to become a mighty church? Why is it important that the church be united and flourishing?

16. Have you ever witnessed severe disagreement in the church or a church split? If so, share the experience. (No names, please!) How might Paul's words in this passage have helped those embroiled in this conflict?

The grand message of Ephesians 2 is that Jesus Christ has destroyed our two great enemies: enmity between God and mankind and enmity between people. Out of this beautiful destruction, God has created a new people, reconciled and unified, as a foretaste of the final unity when Christ returns.   —Sue

God's purpose and Christ's achievement is a single new humanity, a model of human community, a family of reconciled brothers and sisters who love their Father and love each other, the evident dwelling place of God by his Spirit. Only then will the world believe in Christ as Peacemaker. Only then will God receive the glory due his name.
—John Stott (*Message*, 111–12)

 Optional: Read Ephesians 3:1–13.

The following questions are optional, if time permits.

17. In Ephesians 3:1–13, Paul repeats many of the unity principles from 2:11–22. He uses different words, however, to explain these truths. In Ephesians 3:3–5, for example, he uses the word *mystery*. What is the mystery (3:6)?

Recall: In the New Testament, a mystery is a truth that was not understood before but now is being revealed.

18. God called Paul to make this mystery clear to the church (3:8). Who else did God want informed about this mystery (3:10)? Why?

19. According to 3:13, why might the Ephesians be discouraged? What did Paul say to encourage them?

20. How can suffering encourage others and bring glory to God? Have you experienced this? What did you learn about suffering?

Sit Down to Walk

W
e were redeemed and seated with Christ in the heavenlies for a purpose. In the first verse of chapter 4, Paul writes, "As a prisoner for the Lord, then, I urge you to live a life worthy of the calling you have received." Although the NIV translates the word as "live," a more accurate translation is "walk." The next three chapters of Ephesians focus on our walk—the way we live every day.

Are you pleased with your progress in the Christian life? If you died tomorrow, what would people remember? In these chapters Paul describes godly character, and he asks you to pursue these qualities with energy and intentionality. Make them top priority and your lifelong goals! But don't forget—you can only walk worthy when you remain seated in Christ. Let's do a self-examination.

 **Read Ephesians 4:1–16.**

OPTIONAL

Memorize Ephesians 4:2–3

Be completely humble and gentle; be patient, bearing with one another in love. Make every effort to keep the unity of the Spirit through the bond of peace.

All true spiritual experience begins from rest. But it does not end there. Though the Christian life begins with sitting, sitting is always followed by walking. Sitting describes our position with Christ in the heavenlies. Walking is the practical outworking of that heavenly position here on earth.
—Watchman Nee (*Sit, Walk, Stand*, 27-28)

FOUR IMPERATIVES

Verse 1 of chapter 4 contains a connecting word; depending on which version you're using, it might be translated "therefore," or "then," or even "in light of all this." This connecting word declares that everything that follows is founded upon what has come before. As you work through the remaining chapters in the letter, don't lose sight of the necessity of sitting in order to walk or stand. It's easy to do but forgetting to sit unravels everything. —Sue

1. What are the four character qualities Paul mentions first (4:2)? Describe each in a word or phrase.

The Body of Christ is not something remote and unreal, to be expressed only in heavenly terms. It is very present and practical, finding the real test of our conduct in our relations with others. For while it is true we are a heavenly people, it is no use just to talk of a distant heaven. Unless we bring heavenliness into our dwellings and offices, our shops and kitchens, and practice it there, it will be without meaning.
—Watchman Nee
(*Sit, Walk, Stand*, 29)

2. No matter our temperament or bent, we are all called to live out these four qualities. Ask God to reveal, one by one, whether or not these words describe you. Which one is your greatest struggle?

Tomorrow, before you get out of bed, pray that God will enable you to walk in that character quality for the day. Share with the group your progress or frustration. Help one another learn to walk worthy.

3. Next Paul emphasizes the priority of unity in the church. Why is each of these four character qualities so important in maintaining unity?

Here, then, are five foundation stones of Christian unity. Where these are absent no external structure of unity can stand. But when this strong base has been laid, then there is good hope that a visible unity can be built. We may be quite sure that no unity is pleasing to God which is not the child of charity.

—John Stott
(*Message*, 149–50)

4. What is Paul's command in verse 3? Is this your habit? Have you ever caused dissension through a critical spirit, a bad attitude, gossip, or the way you handled a disagreement? Why is unity in the church so important?

5. Why does Paul point out in 4:3 that unity is "of the Spirit"? Although we are instructed to "make every effort," in what way are we powerless to make unity happen?

6. What are the seven "ones" that bond all believers together (4:4–6)? Do you worship with believers who agree with these key doctrinal issues?

SPIRITUAL GIFTS

Now Paul says that although we are called to unity, we are not all uniform (4:7–13).

7. Verse 7 begins with the word *but*. What does that word imply?

As to its essence, a spiritual gift is an ability. It is an ability to function effectively and significantly in a particular service as a member of Christ's body, the church.
—William McRae
(*Dynamics*, 18)

8. In verse 7, Paul proclaims that you are the recipient of something very special that will help you walk and work in the church. Who is the giver?

9. In verses 8–10, Christ is pictured as a conqueror who leads a triumphant procession of believers who fill the whole universe from the highest part of heaven to the lowest part of the earth. What does the conquering Christ give each one of his followers (4:8; 1 Corinthians 12:1, 4–7)?

When my children were growing up, my mission was to make Christmas a special memory for my family. I would spend many hours selecting, purchasing, wrapping, and hiding their gifts. I looked forward to the squeals of delight as they opened them. What if they received them with indifference, or worse yet, never opened them at all? What if they never thanked me for my efforts at expressing my love? I wonder if God feels that way when we are disappointed with our gifts, or worse yet, don't make an effort to discover, develop, and use them? —Sue

10. What are some of the gifts he gave (4:11)? Compare this list with Romans 12:6–8 and 1 Corinthians 12:8–10.

11. Why did he give gifts (4:12–13)?

CORE FOUR

12. Do you know which gift(s) the conquering Christ has given to you? If so, how did you come to that conclusion? What are other ways to know your spiritual gifts?

DIGGING DEEPER

If you do not know your gifts, or would like affirmation, take a gifts inventory. What did you learn? Was this tool helpful?

 Passionate Pursuit (*4:13 minutes*). How has God gifted you for service to him? Learn how Sue discovered her spiritual gifts and how you can discover yours.

13. God created you with natural talents, abilities, and a temperament to complement your gift(s). How do these things work together in your life?

14. If you are aware of more than one gift in your life, are all equally dominant? Do you currently use all of them, or do you find that you use different gifts in different seasons of your life? Which gift(s) are you currently using? Which are dormant? Why?

15. What are some practical ways you can develop your gift(s)?

God has equipped you with spiritual gifts. These gifts are essential to completion in Christ. They help you to function effectively and enable you to mature. They prepare you to be a participator in the work of God rather than an observer.
—Rick Yohn (*Discover*, 3)

DIGGING DEEPER

Are some gifts more important than others? Read and digest 1 Corinthians 12 to learn more about spiritual gifts.

16. Can you think of any dangers in an overemphasis on spiritual gifts? If so, share them with the group.

The gospel frees us from comparison, making it possible to admire other people's gifts and be grateful for their contributions to the Kingdom. In Christ, there is no need for Jell-O molds or rigid constraints. We are called to delight in the diversity that reflects the many facets of God and sheds light on what it truly means to be created in His image.
—Nancy Ortberg
(*Looking for God*, 33)

17. When we all use our gifts, appreciate our differences, and work in harmony, what happens to us individually and as a church (4:13)?

18. What is another benefit (4:14)?

19. New believers are infants and need special care. If you are a new believer, what is a danger you face as a spiritual infant (4:14)? How might you protect yourself? Whether you are a new believer or not, how can you become more grounded so that you will not be easy prey to deceivers? Can you think of an example of when you were "tossed back and forth by the waves, and blown here and there by every wind of teaching"? If so, share with the group

20. In 1 Corinthians 3:1–3, Paul scolds the Corinthians because they should be more grown-up. Would any of his words be appropriate for you? Is there any sense in which you ought to be more mature? If so, identify the areas. Ask God to grow you.

Thank God there are those in the contemporary church who are determined at all costs to defend and uphold God's revealed truth. But sometimes they are conspicuously lacking in love. When they think they smell heresy, their nose begins to twitch, their muscles ripple, and the light of battle enters their eyes. They seem to enjoy nothing more than a fight. Others make the opposite mistake. They are determined at all costs to maintain and exhibit brotherly love, but in order to do so are prepared even to sacrifice the central truths of revelation. Both these tendencies are unbalanced and unbiblical.
—John Stott (*Message*, 172)

21. In verse 15, Paul describes a key character quality of a mature believer. The word *speaking* is absent in the Greek. A more accurate translation is "truthing in love." What do you think this phrase means? Why is this so critical to a healthy church and individual?

22. Do you struggle to walk in truth while exhibiting love at all times? If so, share your frustrations. If not, share your victories.

23. According to verse 15, if you learn to walk both in truth and love, what will happen to you?

24. What will happen to the church according to verse 16? How might your community be affected if all churches were a reflection of verse 16?

25. Read 4:1–16 again. What is the Holy Spirit saying to you? How can you heed the instructions Paul gives you in these verses? Be specific. What do you need to remember as you refine your walk (Ephesians 2:6)?

Tripping Over Your Tongue?
Talk Your Walk!

As a daughter of the King, chosen, rich, redeemed, and seated with Christ in the heavenlies, you are called to walk worthy of your position in Christ. In this section of Ephesians, Paul emphasizes the importance of your words. Pray and ask God to show you the condition of your mouth. James calls your tongue "a fire" and "a restless evil, full of deadly poison." He also says "no human being can tame the tongue" (James 3). He's right! Without sitting in Christ, you will trip over your tongue!

 Read Ephesians 4:17–32.

PAY ATTENTION, PLEASE!

1. How adamant is Paul concerning what he is about to tell you? What is his admonition? (4:17)

OPTIONAL

Memorize Ephesians 4:29

Do not let any unwholesome talk come out of your mouths, but only what is helpful for building others up according to their needs, that it may benefit those who listen.

75

2. How do pagans live (4:17b–19)? Do you know anyone who exhibits these qualities? (No names, please!) What do you observe in this person's life as a result?

OFF WITH THE OLD

Paul's main issue here is transformation—change of identities. . . . "Putting off" and "putting on" are another way of expressing the ideas of dying and rising with Christ. . . . The old being is in a state of ever-deepening corruption and the Christian life is an ever-increasing renewal of the mind.
— John Stott
(*Message*, 234–35)

3. Before Paul begins his instruction on the tongue, he repeats what he told us earlier. Again, he defines the transformation that takes place when one comes to faith. Briefly describe the transformation (4:20–23).

4. Why do you think Paul repeats this truth right before teaching on the tongue?

The putting off the old man and putting on the new man cannot be done by self-effort, nor can it be done by striving to imitate Christ's conduct. It has been done *for* the believing sinner by the death of Christ. We are like babes who cannot dress themselves.
—J. Vernon McGee
(*Ephesians*, 128)

DIGGING DEEPER

What additional insights can you glean from Romans 6:3–14 and 8:1–4 concerning this new life in Christ? What is the only power source strong enough to enable you to walk worthy?

TRUE WORDS

5. What is Paul's first instruction (4:25)?

6. What are some ways believers are false with one another?

7. When are you tempted to be false? Why?

 The Mouth (*3:28 minutes*). Have you heard the phrase "diarrhea of the mouth"? Not pretty, is it? Sue encourages us to cultivate a beautiful mouth.

8. What is the reason Paul asks us in verse 25 to be truthful? What harm can a runaway tongue cause in the church? What happens in a society where deceit becomes commonplace and people no longer trust one another's words?

9. What was Paul's earlier instruction about speaking truth (4:15a)? Why is this imperative?

TAMING DESTRUCTIVE ANGER

10. What is Paul's first command in verse 26? What sins are you likely to commit when you are angry?

Anger is an erroneous zone, a kind of psychological influenza that incapacitates you just as a physical disease would. . . . Anger is a choice, as well as a habit. It is a learned reaction to frustration, in which you behave in ways that you would rather not. In fact, severe anger is a form of insanity.
—Wayne W. Dyer (*Your Erroneous Zones*, 209)

DIGGING DEEPER

Is anger a sin? Is God ever angry? Look up *anger* in a concordance and do a word study on this complex emotion. What do you learn?

11. What is Paul's second command in verse 26? What do you think this means? Share a personal experience if you have one.

12. Why is it so important that you learn to handle your anger appropriately (4:27)? What do you think this verse means?

LESSON 6   79

Anger won't fix itself . . . like a flat tire or a dirty diaper. I remember reading about an eagle that swooped to the ground one day, catching a weasel in its powerful talons. But when it flew away, its wings inexplicably went limp, and it dropped to the ground like a lifeless doll. As it turned out, the weasel had bitten its attacker in midflight, killing the proud eagle as it flew. If we cling to an attitude of anger or jealousy, it will, like the weasel, sink its teeth into us when we least expect it.
—Charles Swindoll (*Tale*, 33)

13. Are you angry often? What angers you the most? What kinds of words came out of your mouth the last time you were angry? If you know healthy ways to deal with anger, please share them with the group.

BUILDING OTHERS UP

14. What does Paul tell the thief to do? Why should you work? (4:28)

15. Earlier, Paul told you that your words must be true. What else should characterize your words (4:29)?

> The tongue is a small part of the body, but it makes great boasts. Consider what a great forest is set on fire by a small spark. The tongue also is a fire, a world of evil among the parts of the body. It corrupts the whole body, sets the whole course of one's life on fire, and is itself set on fire by hell. . . . With the tongue we praise our Lord and Father, and with it we curse human beings, who have been made in God's likeness. Out of the same mouth come praise and cursing. My brothers and sisters, this should not be.
> —James 3:5–6, 9–10

16. Give examples of "unwholesome talk" and of words "helpful for building others up according to their needs." (See also 5:4.)

> I thought such awful thoughts that I cannot even say them out loud because they would make Jesus want to drink gin straight out of the cat dish.
> —Anne Lamott
> (*Traveling Mercies*, 131)

DIGGING DEEPER

Solomon said that the wise use fitting words. What do Proverbs 16:24; 19:5; and 25:11 teach you?

17. Do you struggle with unwholesome words? What could help you in that struggle? If you are an overcomer, help the group.

18. Do you tend to gossip? If you know effective ways to stop gossiping, share them with the group.

19. Uplifting words can build up and heal hurts. Was there a time when someone's words especially encouraged or healed you? If so, please share.

20. What happens when you don't control your tongue (4:30)? What do you think this means?

> We can grieve the Holy Spirit but we cannot grieve him away.
> —J. Vernon McGee
> (*Ephesians*, 132)

21. When did you last grieve the Holy Spirit? How did you feel?

22. Paul ends this passage with a list of emotions and actions that lead to wicked words (4:31). If we eliminate these from our lives, we will likely clean up our conversation. Define each of the following words:

- anger

- bitterness

- brawling

- malice

- rage

- slander

23. What relationships do you observe between these words? Why are wicked words often a by-product? Do any of these actions or attitudes characterize your life?

24. What is the difference between gossip and slander? Why is each so destructive?

So live that you wouldn't be ashamed to sell the family parrot to the town gossip.
—Will Rogers

FORGIVING ONE ANOTHER

25. In verse 32, Paul gives us another key to victory over our words. What is it? How would this heart attitude tend to diffuse destructive emotions that lead to hurtful actions and words?

Why would I forgive someone who doesn't even think she needs to be forgiven? This is why. Because I want my neck and my back muscles to stop hurting, to unfurl like window shades. Because I want to sleep instead of having endless imaginary conversations. Because I want my mind back. Because I want my life back. Because she's not the only one on the hook. Because every time I hang her up on that hook, the hook reaches down and grabs me, too.
—Shauna Niequist
(*Cold Tangerines*, 167)

A believer can never obtain more of the Holy Spirit, for he indwells the Christian's life in all his fullness. But the Holy Spirit can get more of the believer; that is, he can exercise complete control of the life that is yielded to him.
—Alfred Martin ("Epistle to the Ephesians," 1314)

26. Why are we to forgive others (4:32)?

27. What is one thing you can do this week to recapture runaway words? How might your life change if you become a woman whose words are always helpful for building others up?

Walking "Under the Influence"

Paul loved the Ephesians deeply, so he carefully crafted this love letter for them. He knew that if they followed his instructions, they would experience intoxicating joy as a result of their relationship with Jesus. Out of that relationship, they could live well. But he also knew that the only way they could experience this joy was under the influence of the Holy Spirit. In 5:18, Paul wrote the theme verse of this passage: "Do not get drunk on wine. . . . Instead, be filled with the Spirit."

Intoxicating joy is also available to us. But some of us turn to wine or other crutches to help us walk through life. If we do, our hunger and thirst will never be truly quenched. Instead, Paul implores us to place ourselves "under the influence" of the Spirit—because only then can we walk worthy of who we are in Christ.

 Read Ephesians 5:1–20.

IMITATING GOD

1. What are the two things Paul implores you to do in 5:1–2?

OPTIONAL

Memorize Ephesians 5:18b–20

Be filled with the Spirit, speaking to one another with psalms, hymns, and songs from the Spirit. Sing and make music from your heart to the Lord, always giving thanks to God the Father for everything, in the name of our Lord Jesus Christ.

Paul has seen himself seated in Christ; therefore his walk before men takes its character from Christ dwelling in him.
—Watchman Nee
(*Sit, Walk, Stand*, 35)

2. When you were a child, who did you imitate? What impact can role models have on your life?

3. Why should love characterize all you do (5:2)? What is love and how is it exhibited?

4. Are you able to love the way Christ loved? Why or why not? Have you ever loved anyone perfectly? Have you ever spent a day loving others the way God loves us?

5. What is the *only* way you can increasingly live a life of love (Galatians 5:16, 24–25)?

The all-important rule is not to "try" but to "trust," not to depend upon our own strength but upon his.
—Watchman Nee
(*Sit, Walk, Stand*, 38)

The Greek word for sexual immorality is *porneia*, a broad word covering sexual sin, including any form of sexual relations outside of marriage, as well as homosexuality. Greed is added as a separate sin, and can include sexual lust but also refers to any kind of drive to "have more." This was a new standard for most Ephesians since Artemis worship required orgies as part of worship. But God proclaims that bodies made in the image of God are to be treated with the highest reverence and respect, for the good of his beloved. —Sue

DIGGING DEEPER

In the fifth chapter of Proverbs, Solomon warns his son about sexual immorality. Study the text. How might this passage be applied to women as well? If you have a son, how might Proverbs help you train him?

6. Now Paul points out dangerous actions and attitudes. If you adopt these actions and attitudes, you allow the world and the Devil to influence you. What are the first two danger signals mentioned in 5:3?

7. God gave us sexual desires and he delights when these desires are satisfied within marriage. When does healthy sexuality become sexual immorality? What are the particular dangers for women? How can you protect yourself?

8. Why is sexual immorality such a dangerous sin? What are its far-reaching effects?

9. What are special dangers in this information age? How can we protect ourselves and our families from the immoral influence now readily available through technology?

10. In addition to sexual immorality, Paul also warns you to watch out for greed (5:3). Do you struggle with any insatiable desires? How could these desires draw you away from God?

11. Why are sexual immorality and greed especially inappropriate for children of God (5:3; see Proverbs 11:22)?

12. What else grieves God (5:4a)? What heart attitude helps in overcoming the sins of the tongue (5:4b)? Why?

Verses 5–7 can be very confusing. If we do not look at these verses in context or we do not study the words carefully, we might assume that any Christian who is ever immoral or greedy will not go to heaven. But that cannot be true because it contradicts other passages. Ephesians 2:8 tells us our good works did not earn our salvation, so surely our bad works cannot take our salvation away.

Romans 8:1 assures us, "Therefore, there is now no condemnation for those who are in Christ Jesus." And Paul tells us in Romans 8:33, "Who will bring any charge against those whom God has chosen? It is God who justifies." Later in 8:35, he asks, "Who shall separate us from the love of Christ?" and he answers with a long list that makes it clear: nothing can separate us from the love of Christ—not even our own sin nature!

What, then, does Paul mean in Ephesians 5:5–7? First, you must decide whether you think Paul is talking about believers or unbelievers in these verses. There are several reasons to believe he is talking about unbelievers:

1. The Greek word interpreted "disobedient" in verse 6 is *apeitheia*. (See also 2:2.) We get our word *apathetic* from this Greek word. A better translation is "unregenerate" or "unpersuadable," words describing an unbeliever. In addition, the concept of God's wrath is never applied to believers.

2. Paul commands us in verse 7 not to partner with those who are unregenerate, a consistent view with 2 Corinthians 6:14–18.

Verse 4 moves beyond immorality to vulgarity. For *filthiness* means obscenity, and both *silly talk* and *levity* are probably an allusion to coarse jesting, which is the cheapest form of wit. All three refer to a dirty mind expressing itself in dirty conversation. But these *are not fitting. Instead*, Paul says, *let there be thanksgiving*. The contrast is striking and beautiful. . . . The reason why Christians should dislike and avoid vulgarity is not because we have a warped view of sex, and are either ashamed or afraid of it, but because we have a high and holy view of it as being in its right place God's good gift, which we do not want to see cheapened. All God's gifts, including sex, are subjects for thanksgiving, rather than for joking.
—John Stott
(*Message*, 192–93)

3. Paul follows verses 5–7 with a passage contrasting the children of light with the children of darkness, and he addresses his audience as believers and children of light. Believers once were children of darkness, but now they are children of light. Now believers are seated with Christ in the heavenlies, their position in Christ. In the normal Christian life, believers' actions and attitudes reflect their position in Christ more and more as they mature.

4. Throughout the passage, Paul speaks in first person. Then in verses 5–7, he switches to third person, talking about "them" but not "you."

5. There are grave consequences if a believer persists in known sin: premature death (1 Corinthians 11:29–30), being handed over to Satan (1 Corinthians 5:5), and being pursued by the hound of heaven. But hell is not one of those consequences.

Some scholars who argue that verses 5–7 address believers say the answer is found in the interpretation of the word *inheritance*. They argue that believers receive rewards in the kingdom relative to the way they live here on earth. And it is possible for a believer to enter the kingdom without rewards (see 1 Corinthians 3:10–15). A person "who persist[s] in committing such sins as immorality and greed without confession and cleansing (1 John 1:9) would lose his right to rule with Christ in the Kingdom" (Dillow, *Reign*, 72).

 Grace (*4:01 minutes*). Have you accepted God's grace? Do you look for opportunities to pass it on to others? Sue illustrates this beautiful aspect of our faith.

DARKNESS AND LIGHT

13. Again, Paul reminds you of your position in Christ (5:8). What word picture does he use now? What are you to do as a by-product of who you are?

14. Consider the words *light* and *dark*. What do they mean in a physical sense, and what do they mean in a spiritual sense?

Our life is the life of Christ, mediated in us by the in- dwelling Holy Spirit himself, and the law of that life is spontaneous. The moment we see that fact we shall end our struggling and cast away our pretense. Nothing is so hurtful to the life of a Christian as acting; nothing so blessed as when our out- ward efforts cease and our attitudes become natural— when our words, our prayers, our very life, all become a spontaneous and unforced expression of the life within.
—Watchman Nee
(*Sit, Walk, Stand*, 39)

DIGGING DEEPER

Research the concept of light and darkness in John's gospel and letters.

15. Verse 10 tells us *how* to live as children of light. What are practical ways to do that?

16. How are you to relate to darkness (5:11–12)?

17. What does light do to sin (5:13)?

18. Verse 14 is probably a quote from an early baptismal hymn. What is the promise for those who come to faith?

WALKING IN EVIL DAYS

19. With Christ's light shining through you, how does Paul instruct you to walk (5:15–17)?

20. Paul asked the Ephesians to make "the most of every opportunity, because the days are evil." Are our days evil? What are ways we can make the most of every opportunity?

21. What is the command in verse 18? How does alcohol affect you if you drink too much? What are similar spiritual effects when you are "under the influence" of the Holy Spirit?

22. How can you know if you are under the influence of the Holy Spirit (5:19–20)?

23. Do verses 19–20 describe you? Are you drunk with the gods of this world or are you filled with the Holy Spirit? Generally, are you living out your position as a child of the light? Or have you retained actions and attitudes from your dark days? Help one another through sharing and prayer.

> Let no one say that doctrine does not matter! Good conduct arises out of good doctrine. It is only when we have grasped clearly who we are in Christ, that the desire will grow within us to live a life that is worthy of our calling and fitting to our character as God's new society.
> —John Stott (*Message*, 194)

Walk Worthy in Relationships

The people you live and work with every day are usually your greatest relationship challenges. And you are theirs! How do you live worthy of your position in Christ—in the home, church, community, and workplace? Paul teaches you in this passage. Ask the Holy Spirit to help you apply these principles to your life through his resurrection power. Remember, only when you are under the influence of the Spirit can you hope for harmony in your relationships. And remember that your relationships have generational and eternal impact!

 Paul's Bad Rap (*5:11 minutes*). Paul is criticized for expecting wives to submit to their husbands. What's the truth about what Paul had to say?

 Read Ephesians 5:21–6:9.

SUBMITTING TO ONE ANOTHER

1. What is the one overriding principle that affects relationships in life? Why are we to do this (5:21)?

OPTIONAL

Memorize Ephesians 5:21

Submit to one another out of reverence for Christ.

If we are filled with the Spirit, we shall be harmoniously related both to God (worshipping him with joy and thanksgiving) and to each other (speaking and submitting to one another). In brief, Spirit-filled believers love God and love each other, which is hardly surprising since the first fruit of the Spirit is love.
—John Stott (*Message*, 208)

The most difficult part of this text for ancient and modern readers is the expectation that Christians will submit to each other (5:21). Some have argued that mutual submission is illogical, which it is, if viewed apart from Christ. However, if we understand the gospel, mutual submission makes perfectly good sense. What Paul has in mind is that Christians reject self-centeredness and work for the good of others. Submission is nothing more than a decision about the relative worth of others.

—Klyne Snodgrass
(*Ephesians*, 311)

DIGGING DEEPER

Do an in-depth study of the concept of submission in the Bible. In what key areas of life does God ask all believers to live with a submissive attitude? What does this word mean in Greek? A variety of views on submission can be found in Christian literature today. Read about these views. Which do you hold and why?

Verses 21 and 22 must be taken together because the words "submit yourselves" in 22 is not in the original text but has been added by translators. In Greek the two verses are joined together and actually read: *"Submitting yourselves to one another in the fear of God—wives, unto your own husbands, as unto the Lord."* —Sue

2. Define *submission*. What is your gut reaction when you hear the word *submission*? Why do you think you feel this way?

THE WIFE

THE WIFE

3. Who does Paul counsel first (5:22)? How important is a wife's attitude in a marriage, and how does it influence the atmosphere of that marriage and home?

4. What is Paul's analogy in verses 23 and 24? What kind of "head" is Christ?

DIGGING DEEPER

Scholars disagree on the meaning of the world "head" in the Bible. Research this concept. Which view do you hold and why?

5. If you are a wife, do you find submission difficult? If so, why? If you are single and hope to be married, what can you do now to prepare yourself should God bring marriage into your life? If you are widowed, share with the group out of your experience.

Due to the gender confusion ravaging the culture, many seem to perceive that Ephesians 5:22–33 talks about manhood and womanhood. But it's teaching about the mystery of marriage. Ephesians 5:22–33 talks about how the husband should *relate* to his wife and how the wife should *relate* to her husband. The focus of the passage is on becoming one flesh. Oneness has to do with interrelationships.
—Sarah Sumner
(*Just How Married Do You Want to Be?*, 16)

In some places in the first century, wives were considered husband's property and abuse was common. Women were seldom educated, were expected to do what they were told, and were expected to parrot their husband's opinions and ideas. Keep this in mind as you study Paul's countercultural counsel to husbands.

6. Are there any limits to submission? For example, would you counsel a woman to stay in a home where her husband vents his rage through physical abuse (see Acts 5:29)?

Submission has to do with adding to the couple, not subtracting from the wife as a person. When a wife submits to her husband, she does not give up her will. On the contrary, she *exercises* her will to conform her will to her husband's. She does not become a child who obeys him. Rather she chooses, as an adult, to embrace her husband as a means of uniting with him. Submission is not forfeiture. The wife is not commanded to forfeit her perspective or passively give in whenever the couple has a disagreement.
—Sarah Sumner
(*Just How Married Do You Want to Be?*, 90)

7. Does submission to one's husband mean never disagreeing or expressing an opinion? Does it mean becoming a "doormat"?

8. How would marriages and families all over the nation benefit if wives submitted to their husbands as to the Lord?

> Marriage is more than a contract, with partners and stipulations and *if you, then I* arrangements. It's a messy, beautiful, living, breathing thing, full of dreams and history and patterns and memories, and this is the deal: you can make your point all day long, and you can even be right about your point, but if you stop listening, if you stop really hearing and seeing that other person, something fundamental will be lost.
> —Shauna Niequist
> (*Bittersweet*, 221)

THE HUSBAND

9. According to 5:25–27, in marriage, who are husbands to imitate? What did he do for the church? What, then, are husbands to do for their wives?

> Luther seems to have been the first to refer to these lists as household tables or codes. We find these kinds of codes in ancient Jewish and pagan literature, but with one interesting omission. There are no instructions for husbands or masters. Paul was the first to include men in the codes, revolutionizing the relationships in the family for the good of wives and children. —Sue

10. Specifically, how could a husband encourage his wife to be "radiant," "holy," and "blameless" as described in verses 26 and 27?

11. Looking at 5:28–30, how deeply should the husband love his wife? How is he to take care of her? How is the wife protected from abuse or tyranny by these commands to her husband?

12. In 5:31–32, Paul compares unity in a marriage to unity between Christ and the church. What does this imply about the stability and permanence of marriage?

AN ENDURING AND GROWING MARRIAGE

13. How might marriages all over the nation benefit if husbands and wives entered into mutual submission "out of reverence for Christ"?

What does it mean to submit? It is to give oneself up to somebody. What does it mean to love? It is to give oneself up for somebody, as Christ "gave himself up" for the church. Thus "submission" and "love" are two aspects of the very same thing, namely of that selfless self-giving which is the foundation of an enduring and growing marriage.
—John Stott (*Message*, 235)

14. If one spouse refuses to do his or her part, how is the other spouse to respond? Why (see 1 Peter 3:1–2)? Have you ever witnessed or experienced this? If so, please share.

PARENTS AND CHILDREN

The command for children to honor their parents is found five places in the New Testament. The original mandate came from Deuteronomy 5:16 in the Old Testament, one of the Ten Commandments.   —Sue

15. What is the admonition to children (6:1–2)? Give examples. Describe their reward (6:3).

16. What is the admonition to parents, specifically fathers (6:4)? What does this imply about the role of fathers in parenting?

17. Give examples of ways to exasperate children. How can we refrain from this mistake?

18. What does it mean to "bring them up in the training and instruction of the Lord" (6:4)?

DIGGING DEEPER

In Proverbs, Solomon reveals wise principles for raising children. What general principles do you glean? How does Solomon instruct us on discipline? On instruction? On ethics and moral training?

19. In your opinion, do most children today obey and honor their parents, as well as others in authority? Do most parents follow verse 4? What is the result in our families, churches, communities, and nation?

THE WORKPLACE

The next passage teaches the Ephesians how to interact as slaves and masters. Because Paul taught believers to function within this social practice does not mean that God condones slavery any more than he approved of plural marriages in the Old Testament period. In some aspects, these principles can be applied to the employer-employee relationship. There are distinctions, however, between the slave-owner relationship and the employee-employer relationship.

20. What actions and attitudes delight God in the workplace (6:5–7)?

The New Testament neither condones the system of slavery, nor demands its immediate and violent overthrow; but it sowed the seeds of many truths, the growth of which would inevitably bring social slavery to an end.
—Alexander Ross,
("Pauline Epistles," 1029)

21. Even if a paycheck is small, what other benefits can a loyal worker expect (6:8)?

22. How are employers to treat those who work for them? What truth should they keep in mind? (6:9)

23. If you are an employer or an employee, what changes do you need to make as you relate to coworkers? If you work outside the home, what have you learned that might help other women in the group who work outside the home?

24. How would homes and offices be different if everyone wholeheartedly embraced Paul's counsel to "submit to one another out of reverence for Christ"? How would your home or workplace change? Are you under conviction in any of these areas? If so, what will you do?

Sit Down to Stand

Paul has shown us our position in Christ and taught us how to walk worthy of that position every day. In this final section of his letter, he prepares us for "evil days." We have an enemy who wants to destroy us, and, for reasons we usually don't understand, God allows that enemy to attack us from time to time.

If we are not *sitting* with Christ and we have not learned to *walk* with him on a daily basis, we will crumble under these attacks. But through all the resources he provides, we can *stand* no matter what the enemy throws at us! Are you enduring an attack right now? If not, are you ready for an "evil day"? Arming yourself with God's Word today is the best way to prepare for future warfare!

 The Reality of Evil (*4:11 minutes*). Evil is real. But the battle between God and evil is not a battle of equals. What do you need to do when you face off against evil?

 Read Ephesians 6:10–24.

YOUR SOURCE OF STRENGTH

1. What is the command in verse 10?

OPTIONAL

Memorize Ephesians 6:11–12

Put on the full armor of God, so that you can take your stand against the devil's schemes. For our struggle is not against flesh and blood, but against the rulers, against the authorities, against the powers of this dark world and against the spiritual forces of evil in the heavenly realms.

The passive form of the verb ("be strong") indicates that this empowering is something done to Christians, not something they do themselves; its present tense shows the empowering is continual. This is not instruction for a quick fix, but for a life spent drawing strength from Christ.
—Klyne Snodgrass
(*Ephesians*, 338)

2. Our world is obsessed with becoming strong and powerful. Where do many people look for power?

3. According to verse 10, who is the Christian's sole source of strength and power? Describe a woman who looks only to the Lord for strength and power. How does she live?

4. To be strong and stand firm, what does Paul tell you to do (6:11)?

5. In Romans 13:12 and 14, as well as Galatians 3:27, Paul uses the same word picture. From these verses, who is the armor? When did you receive it? Although you possess it, do you sometimes fail to put it on? If so, why?

God has an archenemy, and under his power are countless demons and fallen angels seeking to overrun the world with evil and to exclude God from his own kingdom.
—Watchman Nee
(*Sit, Walk, Stand*, 52–53)

DIGGING DEEPER

What else can you learn about your enemy from the following verses?

· Job 1:6–12
· James 4:7
· 1 Peter 5:8
· 1 John 4:4
· Revelation 20:10

Evil rarely looks evil until it accomplishes its goal; it gains entrance by appearing attractive, desirable, and perfectly legitimate. It is a baited and camouflaged trap.
—Klyne Snodgrass
(*Ephesians*, 339)

YOUR VICIOUS ENEMY

6. Who is your enemy? What do you learn about him from Ephesians 6:11?

7. Often when we encounter adversity and obstacles, we blame people involved. Who is really behind our difficulties? How is he described? Where is he? (6:12)

8. How might an awareness of this reality change the way you respond?

YOUR ARMOR

9. According to 6:13, are you on the offensive or the defensive in spiritual warfare? What are the implications?

10. Have you endured times that you would label "the day of evil"? Describe the experience. What did you learn? How did the experience change you?

11. Verses 14–17 describe parts of the armor. Identify the character quality or spiritual resource that Paul associates with each piece of armor.

    • belt

    • breastplate

    • shoes

    • shield

- helmet

- sword

12. If Christ is our armor, then each part of the armor will reflect a different aspect of his character. Look up the following verses and match each with the piece of armor.

John 14:6a

Ephesians 2:14

1 Thessalonians 5:8b–9

1 John 2:1–2

Revelation 19:11

Revelation 19:13

Every piece of this armor really speaks of Christ. We are in Christ in the heavenlies, and we should put on Christ down here in our earthly walk. Paul has already told us to put on Christ. He is the One who is the truth, and we should put Him on in our lives.
—J. Vernon McGee
(*Ephesians*, 182)

13. If Christ is your armor, then what part does he play in your spiritual battles? Have you tried to be your own armor?

14. Practically speaking, what are some ways to put on the armor of God (6:18; see also Ephesians 1:17; Philippians 4:6–7; 1 Thessalonians 5:16–24)?

15. If Christ is your armor, what do you have to fear? What particular fears do you need to entrust to Christ as your protector, defender, and enabler?

DIGGING DEEPER

For added insight on fear and spiritual warfare, read Psalm 27.

BATTLE PRAYER

16. What was Paul's request in 6:19–20? What part could the Ephesians play in Paul's spiritual battles? In one another's spiritual battles?

17. What part can you play in the spiritual battles that others face? Have you ever been this kind of warrior for others? If so, please share your experience with the group.

PARTING WORDS

18. Who was Tychicus? What was his ministry (6:21–22; Colossians 4:7–8; Titus 3:12)? Have you been a Tychicus to anyone? Has anyone been a Tychicus to you? If so, what is the value of this kind of ministry?

19. How does Paul sign off (6:23–24)? Compare the closing and the opening of the letter. Why the repetition?

DIGGING DEEPER

Read the entire book of Ephesians in one sitting for review. What are the major lessons Paul wants to teach you?

CONCLUSIONS AND ENDINGS

20. In the spiritual life, how is standing different from walking? From sitting? Why does Paul teach these three essential elements in this particular order? What have you learned about sitting, walking, and standing that will make a difference in the way you view yourself and the way you live every day?

God never asks us to do anything we *can* do. He asks us to live a life which we can never live and to do a work which we can never do. Yet, by his grace, we *are* living it and doing it. The life we live is the life of Christ lived in the power of God, and the work we do is the work of Christ carried on through us by his Spirit, whom we obey. Self is the only obstruction to that life and to that work. May we each one pray from our hearts: "O Lord, deal with me!"
—Watchman Nee
(*Sit, Walk, Stand*, 69)

21. What do you think you will remember about this letter five years from now?

22. What will you remember about members of your group? Encourage one another.

Works Cited

Barclay, William. *The Letters to the Galatians and Ephesians*. The Daily Study Bible. 17 vols. London: Saint Andrews, 1958.

Barton, Ruth Haley. *Sacred Rhythms: Arranging Our Lives for Spiritual Transformation*. Downers Grove, IL: InterVarsity Press, 2006.

Beach, Nancy. *Gifted to Lead: The Art of Leading as a Woman in the Church*. Grand Rapids: Zondervan, 2008.

Dillow, Joseph C. *The Reign of the Servant Kings: A Study of Eternal Security and the Final Significance of Man*. Hayesville, NC: Schoettle Publishing, 1992.

Dyer, Wayne W. *Your Erroneous Zones*. New York: Quill, 2001.

Hendriksen, William. *Exposition of Philippians*. Grand Rapids: Baker, 1979.

James, Carolyn Custis. *When Life and Beliefs Collide: How Knowing God Makes a Difference*. Grand Rapids: Zondervan, 2001.

Lamott, Anne. *Traveling Mercies: Some Thoughts on Faith*. New York: Anchor Books, 1999.

Martin, Alfred. "Epistle to the Ephesians." *The Wycliffe Bible Commentary*. Chicago: Moody Publishers, 1962.

McGee, J. Vernon. *Ephesians*. Thru-the-Bible Commentary Series. Nashville: Thomas Nelson, 1991.

McRae, William. *Dynamics of Spiritual Gifts*. Grand Rapids: Zondervan, 1976.

Moore, Beth. *Get Out of That Pit: Straight Talk About God's Deliverance*. Nashville: Integrity, 2007.

Nee, Watchman. *Sit, Walk, Stand*. Wheaton, IL: Tyndale, 1977.

Niequist, Shauna. *Bittersweet: Thoughts on Change, Grace, and Learning the Hard Way*. Grand Rapids: Zondervan, 2010.

Niequist, Shauna. *Cold Tangerines: Celebrating the Extraordinary Nature of Everyday Life*. Grand Rapids: Zondervan, 2007.

Ortberg, Nancy. *Looking for God*. Carol Stream, IL: Tyndale, 2008.

Ross, Alexander. "The Pauline Epistles." *The New Bible Commentary*. Grand Rapids: Eerdmans, 1953.

Schaff, Philip. *History of the Christian Church*. New York: Scribner, 1910.

Snodgrass, Klyne. *Ephesians*. The NIV Application Commentary. Grand Rapids: Zondervan, 1996.

Stott, John. *The Message of the Ephesians*. Downers Grove, IL: Inter-Varsity Press, 1979.

Sumner, Sarah. *Just How Married Do You Want to Be?: Practicing Oneness in Marriage*. Downers Grove, IL: InterVarsity Press, 2008.

Swindoll, Charles R. *Tale of the Tardy Oxcart and 1,501 Other Stories*. Nashville: Thomas Nelson, 1998.

Swindoll, Charles R. *Grace Awakening*. Dallas: Word Publishing, 1990.

Taylor, Barbara Brown. *An Altar in the World: A Geography of Faith*. New York: HarperOne, 2009.

White, John. *The Fight*. Downers Grove, IL: Inter-Varsity Press, 1976.

Yohn, Rick. *Discover Your Spiritual Gift and Use It*. Wheaton, IL: Tyndale, 1980.

About the Author

Sue Edwards is associate professor of Christian education (her specialization is women's studies) at Dallas Theological Seminary, where she has the opportunity to equip men and women for future ministry. She brings over thirty years of experience into the classroom as a Bible teacher, curriculum writer, and overseer of several megachurch women's ministries. As minister to women at Irving Bible Church and director of women's ministry at Prestonwood Baptist Church in Dallas, she has worked with women from all walks of life, ages, and stages. Her passion is to see modern and postmodern women connect, learn from one another, and bond around God's Word. Her Bible studies have ushered thousands of women all over the country and overseas into deeper Scripture study and community experiences.

With Kelley Mathews, Sue has coauthored *New Doors in Ministry to Women: A Fresh Model for Transforming Your Church, Campus, or Mission Field*; *Women's Retreats: A Creative Planning Guide*; and *Leading Women Who Wound: Strategies for an Effective Ministry*. Sue and Kelley joined with Henry Rogers to coauthor *Mixed Ministry: Working Together as Brothers and Sisters in an Oversexed Society*.

Sue has a doctor of ministry degree from Gordon-Conwell Theological Seminary in Boston and a master's in Bible from Dallas Theological Seminary. With Dr. Joye Baker, she oversees the Dallas Theological Seminary doctor of ministry degree in Christian education with a women-in-ministry emphasis.

Sue has been married to David for forty years. They have two married daughters, Heather and Rachel, and five grandchildren. David is a CAD applications engineer, a lay prison chaplain, and founder of their church's prison ministry.